T0162059

UTOPIC

WINNER 2000 BEATRICE HAWLEY AWARD

Other books by Claudia Keelan

Refinery, Cleveland State University Poetry Center, 1994

The Secularist, University of Georgia Press, 1997

UTOPIC

POEMS BY

Claudia Keelan

Alice James Books

FARMINGTON, MAINE

ACKNOWLEDGMENTS

American Letters & Commentary: "Système," "Nearing Trinity"
American Poetry Review: "Zone," "Gravity & Grace," "Blue Diamond," "To the New World," "Calumny's Way"
The Bellingham Review: "Bluff City," "My Twentieth Century," "Nuptial"
Boston Book Review: "Permanently Meadow"
Boston Review: "Again From the Beginning"
Columbia Poetry Review: "Fort-Da," "Toccata With Child"
Denver Quarterly: "Day Book"
Fence: "Oar," "Dust"
Gare du Nord : "Day Book," "Rune"
In*Tense: "Republic"
New American Writing: "Relinquish," "Utopic," "Tactical"
The Journal: "Story," "Oktober"
Volt: "The Beginning of the Golden Age"

"Zone" was also reprinted in the *1997 Yearbook of Poetry and Anthology of Magazine Verse.*

"Utopic," "To the New World" and "Blue Diamond" appear in *The Body Electric,* from Norton.

Alice James Books gratefully acknowledges support from the University of Maine at Farmington and the National Endowment for the Arts.

Alice James Books are published by the Alice James Poetry Cooperative, Inc., an affiliate of the University of Maine at Farmington.

Alice James Books
238 Main Street
Farmington, Maine 04938

www.umf.maine.edu/~ajb

Library of Congress Cataloguing-in-Publication Data
Keelan, Claudia
    Utopic : poems / by Claudia Keelan
        p.   cm.
ISBN 1–882295-28-5
I. title.

PS3561.E3387 U86 2000
811'.54—dc21   00-042394

For Donald and Benjamin

Contents

I.   ZION   1

    My Twentieth Century   3

    The Beginning of the Golden Age   4

    Système   6

    Zone   7

    Oktober   8

    Republic   9

    Fort-Da   10

    Don't Ask Me I'm Not Telling   11

    Tactical   13

    To the New World   14

    Toccata with Child   15

    Utopic   16

II. BLUFF CITY   17

III. BRO.KEN FAC.TOR.Y   31

    Day Book   33

    Gravity and Grace   40

Rune   44

Desert Tract   45

Calumny's Way   46

Nuptial   47

Bray   48

Blue Diamond   49

IV.   THE MEADOWS   51

Story   53

Relinquish   54

Again from the Beginning   55

Permanently Meadow   56

Nearing Trinity   58

Oar   61

Dust   62

Embers   63

Tool   64

Knife   65

Debts   67

Notes   69

I

ZION

"We must take the feeling of being at home into exile.
We must be rooted in the absence of place."

— SIMONE WEIL

MY TWENTIETH CENTURY

It is better   to appear
    untrue   than to *be*   untrue:
    their prayers   a mechanical intonation of a bird.

I   is not a writer
           to serve the cause of language.
The language I knows
            commits errors knowingly,
prayer's language a tool: a cow put to the knife.

The remedy lies in readers,   "Summit Dwellers,"   English,
          despite I's and Our's
          best efforts.

Remedy   commits errors knowingly,
in English,   imitation without
              domination,
Mother-tongue   without imitation:
    "the bowels of the earth"
    "the womb of the earth"
             very sweet
             without domination.
Expression   innocent fun.

Whether construction is permissible or not
prayer/a bird/I on behalf of readers
invite "summit dwellers" say

It is better to appear to
than to be to

THE BEGINNING OF THE GOLDEN AGE

> "In case of doubt, decide in favor of what is correct."
>
> —Karl Kraus

Then she woke up calling an initial
and the dog in the trees,
a calling card in the buchenwald.
The word was elision,
the house creaking, the sun in her eye
then further above, that was good,
elision where the clue was absent,
the Alsatian sniffing the periphery
of vision at the profiteer's boundary.
D shouted, awake and loud,
D absent and the dog,
a localized bullet. *D* elided
but she'd missed the word,
absent, so primary, ab
cess, the wound transforming and infecting you,
elision, like some missed sought for island,
elysian, blond opiate, or
ab
sinthe, a kinder narcotic,
no where but here, in *here* do you feel it,
to nod in, cars through the middle,
the dog gone and the sun
strung through an airplane's wing.
Elision, the will of the mercenary,
the dismembered bodies found by a dog
years later in the dead forest.
Or, the will of the practitioner:
"We give you no God because him
you seek in solitary struggle . . ."
While walking with the children to the train:

"We give you no love, there is no love
without forgiveness, a laborious task..."
Leaving for Treblinka, carrying a gold clover:
I am angry with no one, it is impossible to be so.
Stuttering initials over the snow field
Planting them there
Calling the dog home

SYSTÈME

Let's admit it is open.
And the eye
marking the neighborhood's outline,
faulty. It is open.
Let it be understood, as a general definition,
if "life runs beyond logic"
then the ear, its listening now,
bears the nature of shadow, lace
over a tree trunk.
If it be fair (the shudder of machines
uncoupling on the iron tracks),
it is interesting to observe (making
a sound exactly like murder)
we neither see nor hear them.
If it be fair.
Whereas, the probability of derailment,
the evident, its last cargo spilling and spilling
from the destroyed doors of the train—
We've gone past that for now.

ZONE

Where the small city ended and the desert
was the truer form of mountain
and the fanatic, American angel
threw up his tin horn
swearing a newer, demon love,
I saw the century leave, shivering
in the cargo bin of the newest
merger airline. Things/wings
still mambo as they used,
tho the invisible is stowed
in the pocket of an island native
prancing in dead
policeman's clothes down
the streets of his village.
Something entirely deeper was needed
but the surface remained entirely
surface, studded with light
and travel, those significances
our swiftest means of destination
could neither know nor exile.
Unskilled in linguistics,
the sky is a closed mouth
so the verities, sexual and classist,
belong in your grubby fist,
oh dirty, dirty reader.
Je n'est pas une autre maintenant.
J'attendrai la poche.

OKTOBER

Inside of which the old man walked
surprised by cornices
each day a new angle not seen
before. No atonement OR transcendence,
only approach:
                   THE old man AN old man himself,
the newness of his looking,
hands clasped behind him in habitual
inquiry,
           language's irreparable
backwardness, its continual
substitution of interpretation
for perception.
                  A music box or windchime,
inside or out, psychosis and soul:
                        a code losing the ability
                        to decode.

Inside a season lately.
Leaves all over the wall.

REPUBLIC

I'd rather your mind's quagmire
    than the terribly close
frailty of body nothing
    much less me could
press upon. However thin,
    so thin, you were cheerful,
chastising your poverty
    on prime time, signing over
your checks, believing in generation,
    etc. No complicity
between us, no ingrained
    loneliness, I could not love you.
You were a nation without me.

FORT-DA

What was white was white then disappeared completely.
Hovering all my life and gone.
Lonely for oppression, oppression lonely,
a blind boy running very fast on a treadmill.
A century of moral fiction,
generosity and genius slipped their root.
A basket, an overhead light.
Word ugly.
I loved her that way.
Heavy snow. Fall down.

DON'T ASK ME I'M NOT TELLING

There's no filling anything,
bag of sick,
briefcase full of the dead sea.
It's easy to comprendre, Ramon Perez,
everyone's tired of it,
have you seen me?
The Jiffy Lube time simulator
drawing exactly the face of Juan Perez
seven years after you stole him.
The God on fire in dreams and in days,
the red surge *there* and *there*,
laughing at you, at me.
Take me for instance,
an animal fingering hunger runes,
the carousel horses my boy
refuses to ride
ascending behind my closed lids
until his absence is complete.
Draw *that* Jiffy Lube, you fucker,
time's on your side but nothing else.
Raymond and John are far from the sea
and I've stopped following them.
And the next, oh, the next,
I lost my nerve there and there
my love's dead sister
still sits in the front row of the Christmas pageant
a child, her last second written on her brow.
Nobody goes farther than that,
take me for instance,
Ramon, Juan, my boy,
the world I can't fill in,

quiet beneath a horse's tongue.
Need gets used up in it.
Mothers, fathers, lose the thread,
the senile's "is that you grandpa?"
to her youngest son
and why not,
why not, there's nothing here
to tell us where we are,
Jiffy Lube, poetry,
calligraphy of present and past.
I should know and I won't tell,
all my faces in this ruined future.

TACTICAL

You wanted me for my noun and then you wanted me general.
Militarily, but without the movement towards
the Front: mostly Western, saleable, over.
       Inside history.
As sex stops thought
       of sex and thought
stops fact of mind:
       They were engaged.
I, on the other hand, was peopled by absence.
Agamemnon was dead. Another tried
       but he was not Ulysses
and when he cried on a street in Sarajevo
       counting the bodies of the dead
a Front in me Grew a face,
       carried a sign:
       No passengers.
Lose. From every stone, *Lose.*
All that evocation. You who have not known
marriage, the terror of good fortune: **stop searching forever**
happiness is just next to you.
       Writing began with counting,
a scribe numbering life, refusing objects and names.

TO THE NEW WORLD

Saturday grieves
           Puritan seeking *more weight*
Machines look unhappy in the desert
           "you can't tell <u>me</u>
<u>he</u> didn't do it"
           no one there and it's true
Her hands against the window
Her breath
The empty backs of trucks are screaming
what more do you want from me
I'll be as clear as I can
My son <u>knows</u> the puddle is an ocean
Our camera killed Her
He fell by himself
Imperfection is everywhere. I wear her star.
Africa is a long scar in my head.
Sad grass.
Lovely mud ocean.
I'm seeing a world, no, a room, or
           a space like a musical phrase
princess, sister/s'aint & tribe
           imperfect under funeral flowers
P/ity   Merc (I) (Y)   Peace
           &
           luve

All alone in our boats

TOCCATA WITH CHILD

I came in from under the music
a Thursday
far to go etc. pulling out all the stops
until Sunday when it started again
in five voices
and I saw I was a woman
feeding her son
on the inside, somehow,
(a Thursday)
everything but nothing
pushing against the shape I made
(a woman) bent towards an open mouth
specific hunger calling the day
I wanted to wake in
listening to cacophony
and then I heard no longer
(until Sunday) when it started again
in a single voice
and I saw everything but nothing
in the (specific hunger) small body
asking me to *wake up* and listen
from Thursday and each
day (until Sunday) and starting begins again
I hear it, small specific body,
inside (a door slams) somehow hungry in the music playing
in all the stops

UTOPIC

The pressure of being/of more than one
        Oh Celebrators,
the world winding towards nothing/
        may I say nothing
Rue de Fleurus
                Hope of the pear
Because there is not eating
QUEL Q'UN:
Maintenant, oui   there is hope
& Now   there is no room for
                          far away emotion

What is social moves
        with delayed hooks
toward compromise

Imagine his head wounds
        Oh Christendom
Impresario   dying exile
        Take notes:
In the wind the dog's cries
    are the dying Martin

The emotion away from emotion
    a service not a method

A generation slipping nouns
If you say it that way
        Noose March Law

11

BLUFF CITY

"the same indignation that is said to have cleared the temple
once will clear it again...it seems as if no one had ever died in
America before; in order to die you must first have lived . . ."

— HENRY DAVID THOREAU
Plea for Captain John Brown

But it still doesn't explain why

                it took the passive

resistance form it took.

                I was eight when he died in this city.

Dying on the outside, the gunshot

                of that year killing the inside

of what constitutes my/our

                "The method is passive physically

but strongly active spiritually."

                In that I had a way of seeing

attached to my feeling

                paralyzed at the beginning

of Being.

                "It is not the suffering

but that which comes from outside

                which is remedy."

(the method)   (the paralyzed will)

(of a child)   (of a nation)

"We talked about it in India

                and in Africa but the American

movement was—
unpremeditated, a natural,

                a religious."

(meant staying inside)   (a child)

(inside)   (a nation)

In that I had a way of seeing

where the world wouldn't start

(inside a child nation)

dead.'"
"It is not the suffering

which is remedy."

(a child)

"And the other thing is

already, the Negroes

anyway, responsible."

is passive,

are always active."

of Being.

attached to my feeling

immobilized

"Then Moses said 'the kids are

but that which comes from outside

The kids are dead.
(of a nation)

people were being killed

of Mississippi and I feel,

"For while the nonviolent resister

his mind and emotions

At the beginning

"Writers themselves always try to lessen the distance between their kind and ordinary human beings. They so often assure us that every one is at heart a poet and that the last poet will not die until the last human does."

In that I had a way of seeing

attached to my feeling

and when I couldn't *see* to feel,

I ceded the day to event.

Or I lost the trajectory

of the hours

huddled in a stingy minute

thought in a sound loop

the music all wrong

tho I'd given it away, my feeling

willingly, by the handful.

History is the gap

through which the lessons fall:

"Moses said 'the kids are dead.'"

In that I had a way of seeing
attached to my feeling
but the dead bird, just there and there
until I picked it up with a shovel
and buried it
in the street.
            Its end written already, a thousand worms a coat
or jeweled shroud so that the leaves I pushed
over what remained of its body
seemed unholy or I did,
performing last rites without the benefit of a bell or veil,
empty of blessed words. A false priest with a shovel
an evening falling/an evolution of the bodiless
/the decayed interior of a bird
the medium where I began to understand:

when he hit her
      bringing the heel of his hand down
across the bridge of her nose
      it's safe to say he felt her skin
as an extension of his own
      the slight pop the bones made shattering
hardly in competition with the sirens, the flight patterns
      much less the—roaring? or simply the language?—
of his psyche, because he was all inside, he must have been,
      ignoring the streetlight, the dogs and other people
walking and then shouting, his hand, that instrument rising
      almost detachedly, higher and higher
until the force was clean and attached to intention.
      There is no safety in *saying.*
The wallet then almost a distraction
      and the way he ran away
"trying to lessen the distance between"
      (loping, looking over his shoulder)
"their kind"
      (soul depicted)
"and ordinary human beings"
      at the heap she made in the street.
Two boys skate over the spot today.
      A black man they say
and they're ready for him
      holding tree branches in their hands.
It's warm and green shows in the brown.
      When I look again
they've tied the sticks together
      and are sailing into town.
Bluff City.

Even without the windows open
            I've been dreaming
behind bars that face the neighbor
            my sleep has made
whole again.
            I've resisted his story,
hurried inside to stop him
            depicting the apparatus
of event and time
            that left his body crushed
from the shoulders down.
            He believes
that touch, in Japanese,   R

                            E

                            I

                            K

                            I
can keep you in this world
            and a nurse has slipped into mine,
simply the word "nurse"
            and the hands she lay
on his forehead
            15 years ago.
(Who believes in touch cannot)
            (who cannot believe must)
I am reading the underlined
parts of HEAL YOUR BODY
by Louise L. Hay he slipped
onto my porch:

5-C Fear of ridicule and humiliation   *I lovingly release others to their*
                                          own lessons.

Fear of expression.
Rejecting one's good.   *I lovingly care for myself.*
Overburdened.   *I am loved.*
                                          And I am safe.

In the dream I might have had
he has reclaimed his name, Butch,
and he and the two boys
drive three to a cab,
two sticks, a gun and the intentionality
of a city,
fuschia scripture
mending earth to sky.
(God bless what is broken, what cannot move,
God bless the reflection that is harmless
unattached to desire,
the minor delusions
that strengthen our humanity)

Lessen the distance

In that the outside disappeared completely
into the limbs of his body
so that when I see him in his chair in the sun
I know that it's day.

No dream possible
            he's back (we're
back), or a version of us
            "looking into your window with a knife" or further
down the street
            "back from the army and looking for a friend."

Something subdued,
            halted in the weightlifter's
                        STOP THERE OR I'LL SHOOT
(I'm not kidding)
                        In the neighborhood's WATCH GROUP,
the names, the numbers we exchange.

Night in the flight patterns the steamboat
crying the violence turned
outward and upstairs, his cry/her cry
mine/the small boy's/night of the wheelchair
and the eyes he turns
to the stars at the end of the drive.
Night of nothing seen or felt,
the cries protracted in the spine
and the silence, the aftermath
protracted and protracted,
the whole body fed by it,
severed by the sleeping child.

The religion in expression,
        true or false. Religious tanks
moving up Poplar Avenue,
        religion of curfew,
the monuments to memory
        something wants to wreck.
The moot dismemberment
        of Christ *again*,
in her arms, in Rome
        so you see now there is nothing
left to recall but the shape
        they write in the body.
Genetics suffering history,
        cattlecar lowing towards
the museum. All the responsible pictures
        promising your children
sitting, or standing, a place on the train.
        I would like to invite you to lunch
I am your age
        The world is a place I would like to step off of
There is forgetting to do
        in my church
Been disabled,
        enjoy I think, common interests?

"You asked what happened to Rosa.
I think I can tell you.
You know the law
you say, well,
let's fight it.
It's that. That's
just the whole attitude.
A time when you decide you don't give a rap.
I don't live in_____
but I'm in _____
and I know why people fell in."

(a child)   (of a nation)

She walked alone.
            (at the corner)(I tried to pass)
(through)   (the guards the crowd)   (was quiet)
            (I tried to squeeze)   (past him)
(they raised his)   (bayonet)   (and they raised their)
            (bayonets)   (somebody yelling lynch
and lynch her)   (Drag her to the etc.)
            (the branch seemed safe to me)   (a white lady)
(very nice)   (put me on the bus)   (a white man)
(patted me) (raised me) (said don't let them
            see you cry.)

But it still doesn't explain why
it took the passive
resistance form it took

                                          (I tried to squeeze) (past)

We talked about it in India
and in Africa but the American movement was—
        unpremeditated, a natural, a religious. Over.

(And he raised his) (And they raised their)

I had not begun not believing

        in a center, a self's

or this city's but thinking

        to make one or find

one or only to find

        one in the making.

What I love

        I left singing

in the student gallery,

        the elevator rising

away from the music I continued

        to hear until I stepped off

in another place.

        You divisible in the notes

you whistled among the bad

        sculptures and I—

feet traveling a hallway. Song forgotten

        and the elevator's ascent away

from what you had become—only a point,

        not fixed, but a *point*—not ever

a place to return to.

        This city's quick descent

to the Mississippi not a simile

        for anything related to us,

as the bridge cannot

        be a freedom stretching west

from the city of two dead kings

        where last night the sun

fell into the river and shared

        its light a while before

it went away.

The method is passive physically but strongly active spiritually.
(I tried to pass)   (was quiet)
The aftermath creation of the beloved
(and he raised his(and they raised their
And aftermath creation of endless bitterness
(patted me(raised me(said(don't let them
see you

I hadn't known it would be a motel
on the edge of Memphis, turning away until he said, no, there.
                              The Lorraine Motel, Rm. 306,
a wreath over the number
we were forced by the architecture
to start on the outside,
to start at the end
of Martin's life, the well photographed
balcony leading

                              se
                                quence of
                              a a meta
                                  morphosis of the
                              vis oral   cul
                                          ture and religious
                              tradition
                              to insure the retaining of an
                              a leg   acy

in nerve, in language on to Rosa's bus
and the inside of his room,
artificial coffee memorialized in black plastic
If there is no struggle there is no
          progress   Am I not a sister

Memphis, 1996

29

III

BRO.KEN FAC.TOR. Y

DAY BOOK

I.

Inside it   a blessed sickness
       subsided   and what was   body
convulsed   soul

Inside it   a darkness   sudden wind
       lifting   my face   towards name
    found   it could live   comfortably

Irresistible,   the first days   sentiments
       out here   in these *periods*   of mentality
well being   always head

       Inside   a trace of it   now

2.

A church burning   the not again   again
    race devours   the radio
God the pilot   a tuneable   metal?

Animal shadows   devour   Your hillside
    The not again   American city
burns race burns   church
                   without ceasing   without

A pilot's broken   radio   lost
    Lost words   an ocean
Inside animal shadow   inside   Your hillside

3.

I construct it	without color	by grief & simper
It was golden		smoke
stems weakly erect	yellow flowers	shorter
	than leaves	

Rock held you   were not wise   won't return
       tho gold   smoke her body
more lasting   yellow flower   yellow soul
                       won't return

Body smoke   Her smoke   return
       Not yours, Margaret   I knows
Too well   who is gone   I looked in the coffin
                       She was there

More lasting   than return

For Margaret Keelan Kerley, 1921–1996

Suffering must be outward to be redemptive. When I say "I suffer" only then does "I" become instructive, activated by speech. But speech alone isn't enough.

The beloved community is born from an all inclusive definition of itself: it is a room or field, hallways or alley, a *place* which encloses struggles between justice and injustice—room, raum, stanza, cuarto, place—a *word* containing the forces of light and the forces of darkness. And still, the revolution is of One, as regards the internal force, the Enthusiasm, and the apparatus to which one unites her suffering, e.g. Gandhi's entry into jail as "a bride groom enters the bride's chamber."

: The beloved community becomes peopled then with opposing selves using words to confirm Justice, Light, etc. *within* their separate internalities (enthusiasms). Language, the apparatus of suffering, in service of community rooms, resolutions and the love of lovers.

5.

Wrote
    wrote
-ion

And *there* is Beloved
    wrote
being nearer
        approaching

an end here, beloved
        in
singing
        Being nearer

"citizen"
"constitution"
Comes an end
& others

wrote
the body

the politic
we did not know
wrote music

in the book
the body of a convict
to Her

Citizen
a conviction
or nearer
or approaching

A beautiful bird
it was early and
but felt
in Her hair

6.

To extend lyric

to include the gaps

(what I feel brushing its breath, wings, breath,

its *material* between

the limits of two letters)

Being neare<u>r</u>   <u>o</u>r nearer

   approachin<u>g</u>   <u>o</u>r approaching

Children and savages   use nouns   & names
              where is savage?   & convert
into verbs   *savage savage*
              All is savage

In this paradise   (stay with me)
              There is nothing to frame
Wind savaging   a desert
              wilding it, right   Those children
in Central Park,   *naturing* right   Beating Her & Beating
Her &   Oh but the wind is spirit,
savage construct   The desert and I open her eyes
              Freedom as far as far can

GRAVITY & GRACE

I.

À fin   all was strange   of my heart
    a landscape   of I am not
Disappearing, things   became perfect

Once   to hear, see, touch   eat
    deprived God   something saying   I,
a landscape   disappearing   in I am not

Now perfect,   disappearance   appearing perfect
    see hear   *sear*   touch not
a landscape fin   in I   of I am not

2.

If my window   is red   I cannot see
        anything   but rose   accord
to rose   the window   to revolt

Mountains, rocks   fall upon us   Hide us
        far   I deserve this   wrath
the red principle   of revolt   the rose

Room the red window   Violence
        trains view   Mountains, rocks   fall
train wrath   Tho I die   doing

3.

Suffer	suffering	to reduce it
Not sacred enough	Being and others	
Rock upon	the obstacle	the rock

Suffering spread	beyond reduct	-ion
Sacred good	or beautiful thing	an insult, then
Being inside rock	transformed mud	& others

Forgive	the void beautiful	in being
a branch	to a drowning	future
Sacred enough	or not	Writing

forgiveness

4.

Good broken up into   pieces
       a host of women   or of men
I leaves marks   on the world it destroys

Broken good   never anything *new*   everything
       equivalent   a host of   /or of
I was your friend   once

Lost Her   knowing good but hating good
       She broke into   equivalent pieces
I held Her   lost good

In a broken   factory   a single tear
       destroyed Host   and Host
                           I destroyed
preserving Her

RUNE

In Hainesville, Alabama   Jonathan Daniel
     military cadet attaining
          CIVILIZATION   (L) CITIZEN
dies 1965

                 & Ruby Sales lives to Priesthood
                 Canterbury, 1997
     The resurrection window fills with his name

Citizenry wars   do not end
       Jonathan Daniel
unarmed citizen   takes Her bullet
       Hainesville
              & in Canterbury Cathedral
              Her dark face & priest robes
     Resurrection fills our name

A martyr is   witness
              & somebody who
is not prepared to compromise
           Our faith

    Jonathan Daniel

DESERT TRACT

Wrongs authored nature,
      my country.
I's sensible of decline.
Music's definiteness for example.
The delay, prompt, the beat
as much a container as sight.
Put fingers over the holes.
Sound's suffering escapes.
Even duration's a wounded thing.
Duration's nature rights
wrongs, authors holes.
Power escapes!
Beating the container, prompting
      the animal's
pain. Suffering delays sound,
music's indefiniteness is example.
Sight, my country, in holes.

CALUMNY'S WAY

First it was sex
        and then it was God,
the fire from one
        lending self to the other.

And then, oh, the world. Civilian days in long tubes, companionship of
poster children and final viruses. Sex whispered in the threshold. God
was a calf's eye, a small extended belly. C-I-V-I-L-I-A-N.
I memorized the image.

In the past that is, the black dog
        lays his head all day in my lap.
He is clean as dirt and needs me.
        This is Furnace, the grasshopper's song
& sex & God are one.

I eat my animal and am done.

NUPTIAL

I's   not an   altar
    a bride   raised on earth
Wild grass   grows over bodies

Yearning   roots   th'eye
        & I   grows   a bride
Looks & sees   not   Looks & sees

Seeds   th' inner impulse of th' tree
        wild grass   in the bride
The bodies   inside I

BRAY

Love wretchedness   God loves
               something else
Love for us   is reason
               Love for us   is us ourselves

Blindfolded   chained to a stick
               I explores   means of it
I feels oneself   the stick
               Oneself   a stranger

Metallic coldness   Love
               made metal   made violence
The stick   I feels
               Oneself   made metal

Love passed   through fire
               made Us   made I
a stranger   oneself   a stick

BLUE DIAMOND

I am virtually gone
                              author or victim
I wanted   in you   to be nothing
        to be a solitude
attached   by emptiness   to everything

Last night   one coyote
                        this morning two   They were nature

Keep the children close
                        author or victim
The desert looks flat, lies
        flat   what does realism save?
They were animals running across the surface
They are gone

IV

THE MEADOWS

"The angel and apostle of the coming revelation must be a woman, indeed, . . . lofty, pure, and beautiful; and wise, moreover, not through dusky grief, but the ethereal medium of joy . . ."

—NATHANIEL HAWTHORNE

STORY

I am living at your back
surrounded by boxes
and a thin layer of dust
obscuring the labels,
the destination of things.
Something is holding us up
in our sickness; that is,
I can see you're still sitting upright.
I live behind our lives,
problematic outlook.
What cannot stop arriving
huddles in the lap between us.

RELINQUISH

The real world was inaccessible
to us *noumenon, noumenon.*
Not only not real
but not significant,
noumenon, noumenon.

The end of the century THE MEADOWS,
end of THE MEADOWS
a desert, vision itself
a mirage, *noumenon,*
noumenon. The Illusionist

leashes his tiger. The Illusionist
is his tiger. You think
    to resist it
noumenon, noumenon?

You vanished an hour ago.
What is lost
in many windows.
Roaring fogging the glass.

AGAIN, FROM THE BEGINNING

Love hangs a sign
written in huge letters
but your mouth won't form the words.
The right places never held meaning
and though you knew life
wasn't art, you wanted it to be:
the confessional too easy a box
to enter and leave or East
becoming solidly *East* because the map said so.
Not understanding
but acquiescence to form. Flowers on a tomb.
The cars passing and then gone
along the avenues suggested a moral
equation you had to follow
to know. The yellow hills made you lose
heart, but the sounds of pity
heard through the intercom in the broken
tongue of your city!
You'll never translate them,
but you are tracing
their shapes in the palms of hands.
You are recognizing their signature
on the calligraphed backs
along the interstate
and in the meaningless body America
promises at each exit.
You cannot get home.
You have not done your job.

PERMANENTLY MEADOW

Nothing ever so personal
as everyone else's story:
$\qquad\qquad\qquad$ They said it was brilliant
the way the country drive
eluded the country drive
$\qquad$ *stay here* $\qquad\qquad$ *stay here.*
A half smile of a mistimed child.
A halo immigrant.
Who cares *what's* in Her freezer,
she's our mother.
Never tender about old ice/meat gravy,
even tho Johnny thought he was funny,
the approval She withheld
paving the way to the meaner joke,
the one at, you know, anyone who's
listening's expense.
Swallowing nightlamps//pledging inattention:
As, in the long stretch of daylight
headlight testing area,
you lift your eyes to the yellow
$\qquad\qquad\qquad$ FALLING ROCK
and it's a sign for a rock falling—
not the Hidden Indian of childhood—
for real now, or nothing;
Or, as the cars your brother slammed
your arm for misnaming,
oh Mustang, hair matted, there
alone in a wash, oh
Mustang, so wild and so
defunct tho' herds
of government butchers
lure you towards the glue arena;

Or, as the city that opens
the doors of simile
at last in a red silver tinkle,
as Elvis, *as* Marilyn, New York
and Freedom,
I lay my straw hat before you,
fathers, fathers, fathers,   faith of mine, not
what is slow dreaming
curled inside me   speaking.

NEARING TRINITY

1.
"it's only earth's body"

                                    "His Highness Mourning"
in the wind.

Man, Man?
Daddy says God, then Earth's body.

I say fuck you
and pity me and if night is dust and bad sound
then day is a crane where the sky once was.

I can, I'm a meadow.
And if you're forced to be a pilgrim,
I prove every wandering person
according to the texts,
the billboards who lay their wreaths.

No beneath
only blue glass
and nothing of you whatsoever there.

Only earth's body from the darkness.

Harder and older.
Almost unbearable.

2.

sage no longer
      tread   tread
                                I try to believe in my son's flesh,
one hand on the Dead End sign,
another pulling a wooden snail.
Desert land,
      razed hardpan—
My language can't reach his life.

The single flower Donald finds,
puts on the table—

Minuscule beauty,
      V-I-O-L-E-T

All the world's body opposes a frame, framed.

When Benjamin asks who I was

will I acquiesce to form,

come to believe in the past,

hand him *this*?

3.

A dove uncoupling a train,
I confused my God with my animal.
That was waste nothing could contain.
Infected light bodying her serious amour,
scree scree   coo coo.
Deus ex machina   Holy game,
Me? Me?

                Oh yes   Oh no

and all ungendered

coo coo   scree scree

OAR

I had wanted to describe the river but
    away   in the distance   on two sides
                    see the banks.

The river fills the propellers.   Neither the river
    nor the ship is mine & in the distance
                    see the banks.

The virtue I wants is none.
Confession is a broom,
the surface cleaner than before.
I wears my fellows beings,
the surface stranger for confession.

The pages amply prove repression
                is violence,
the pages in prohibited areas,
              violence.

I's disobedience is a preparation
    for more suffering
      unperceived   gentle
homage to ourselves.

DUST

Be prepared to suffer cheerfully.
Reduced in body
spirit greeted:
          "Are you nearly dead?"
Brightness had made hunger.
Deprived of
          & of,
Being could not
afford to eat to live.
Cheerfully reduced,
Brightness made food of deprivation.
Being could not.
Everyone who has experience
          knows they are most starved.
Of does.
& does.

2.
Spending human labor,
dis-ease a lapse,
a physical gospel.
Make most sentences indeterminate,
sketch barest outline.
Dis-ease, human, a labor,
          a physical gospel,
honesty at a discount.
Its barest outline
sketches experience,
most starved.

EMBERS

Apologize for birth &
       convey more being.
What is true outside
is equally true inside.
Apologize and convey.
Believe unprovoked suffering
       speaks unrivaled,
silent suffering
       speaks unrivaled.
It is solid work   it is always true

TOOL

The one I wanted to teach
                                    proved to by my teacher:
Christ's sermon on the mount,
                Buddha, with the lamb on his shoulder,
                        love at heart.
The one I wanted to teach
                                    silenced spirit,
dharma guru   wind erasing all edge.
No one follow me.
The slaughter house is in the heart I pass.
Beautiful spots in that place & there countless are killed,
my idea of devotion.
Follow ideas   Christ's sermon on the mount,
Buddha, with the lamb on his shoulder.
        Love at heart
        requires understanding.
The slaughter in the heart I pass,
knows no other method.

KNIFE

The power to die   everyone has.
     The weak   cling to life.
A black ant,   its leg broken,
     dragged a child very hard.
Her parents let go her hand.
Suffer this cost.

I'm ashamed of Being   a man,   a woman,
     born an enemy of Mother,
     only to remain slaves.
Hope limits purity.

The power to die   everyone has.
     The weak   let go Her hand.
     If one is oneself so is the world.
     Suffer this cost.

Debts

"Je est un autre" is still the largest proposal ever made, long before and af-
ter Rimbaud's beautiful sentence, by Jesus, Simone Weil, Martin Luther
King Jr. and many others. It is too simple, it is too complex, its concept
of unity suffused with the agony of disunity, suffused with the single im-
perative of meeting oneself *in* oneself and *in* the other. Just as saintliness
is unnatural in the willing mortification of the flesh, and passive resis-
tance is unnatural in its acceptance of pain and death for the betterment
of the whole, so there is in the violation of language's conventions, a
wholly unnatural inclusiveness to be forged. Method as a means and end
unto itself is an instrument of hallucination; Gandhi's urging people to
accept the repeated blows of the British seems an act diabolical at worst,
irresponsible at best, without the ideality of Indian equality he believed
would result from the act. Similarly, experiments with breath, noun,
pronoun, tense, case, punctuation, etc. must not be experiments inter-
ested only in the "materiality" of language, but experiments dedicated to
finding, at the level of the syllable, what *life* has been left out or erased in
dominant culture's acceptance of conventional language modes. Such
poetry is made of notes, without hierarchical but strictly relational value,
a poetry whose ethos, like music's, is indiscriminate in the best sense. In-
side of it, a center is ever emerging, a center which is, nonetheless, rooted
in the song's initial movement; its sense accrues in what is added—and
erased—from its original motif. Inside of it, the true is ultimately impro-
visational, but is the original impulse. Just as King's aim in accepting im-
prisonment was to de-center, to de-stabilize status quo by calling existing
hierarchies into question—; as Simone Weil's refusal of the designation
Jew was the beginning of a secular and religious experiment that still dis-

turbs orthodoxy; as Gandhi's lifelong commitment to destroy the designation "untouchable" written into his religion made him suspect in the Indian world; so the degree to which such poetry succeeds will depend upon an addition to—and erasure from—existing definitions of poetry.

Las Vegas
2000

Notes

The quoted passages in "Bluff City" are freely adapted from several letters and essays of Martin Luther King, Jr. compiled in *Black Protest*, New York, Harper and Row, Publishers Inc, 1968, as well as Sigmund Freud's essay "Creative Writers and Daydreaming."

The quoted passage in "The Beginning of the Golden Age" is freely adapted from "Janusz Korczak: A Tale for Our Time," in Bruno Bettelheim's *Freud's Vienna & Other Essays*, Vintage Books, 1991.

In "Relinquish" I use *nuemenon* in its philosophical designation "the truth behind appearances."

"Day Book" is a loose orchestration of Ralph Waldo Emerson's letters and "Gravity and Grace" is an homage piece to Simone Weil. The reader is welcome to sing along in the empty spaces.

"Nuptial" is an argument with Confucius.

"Oar," "Dust," "Embers," "Tool," and "Knife" owe their lives to the writing of Gandhi.

Recent Titles from Alice James Books

Pity the Bathtub its Forced Embrace of the Human Form,
  Matthea Harvey
Isthmus, Alice Jones
The Arrival of the Future, B.H. Fairchild
The Kingdom of the Subjunctive, Suzanne Wise
Camera Lyrica, Amy Newman
How I Got Lost So Close to Home, Amy Dryansky
Zero Gravity, Eric Gamalinda
Fire & Flower, Laura Kasischke
The Groundnote, Janet Kaplan
An Ark of Sorts, Celia Gilbert
The Way Out, Lisa Sewell
The Art of the Lathe, B.H. Fairchild
Generation, Sharon Kraus
Journey Fruit, Kinereth Gensler
We Live in Bodies, Ellen Doré Watson
Middle Kingdom, Adrienne Su
Heavy Grace, Robert Cording
Proofreading the Histories, Nora Mitchell
We Have Gone to the Beach, Cynthia Huntington
The Wanderer King, Theodore Deppe
Girl Hurt, E.J.Miller Laino
The Moon Reflected Fire, Doug Anderson
Vox Angelica, Timothy Liu
Call and Response, Forrest Hamer
Ghost Letters, Richard McCann
Upside Down in the Dark, Carol Potter
Where Divinity Begins, Deborah DeNicola
The Wild Field, Rita Gabis
Durable Goods, Suzanne Matson
This Particular Earthly Scene, Margaret Lloyd
The Knot, Alice Jones
The River at Wolf, Jean Valentine

ALICE JAMES BOOKS has been publishing exclusively poetry since 1973. One of the few presses in the country that is run collectively, the cooperative selects manuscripts for publication through both regional and national annual competitions. New authors become active members of the cooperative, participating in the editorial decisions of the press. The press, which places an emphasis on publishing women poets, was named for Alice James, sister of William and Henry, whose gift for writing was ignored and whose fine journal did not appear in print until after her death.

TYPESET AND DESIGNED BY MIKE BURTON

PRINTING BY THOMSON-SHORE